ALBERT SCHWEITZER

by James Bentley

2/90
Champion 12.45

Picture Credits

Albert Schweitzer Archives, Günsbach, France, pp. 7, 12-13, 14, 17, 18, 20, 21, 24, 32-33, 34 (both), 35, 52; (c) Erica Anderson photographs by courtesy of the Albert Schweitzer Center, Great Barrington, Massachusetts 01230, USA [Telephone (413) 528-3124], pp. 4, 8, 10, 11, 23, 28, 29, 37, 42, 43, 44, 46, 47, 48, 49, 53, 54, 56, 58, 59; Ardea, p. 40; Bildarchiv Prussicher Kulturbesitz, p. 27; GSF Picture Library, p. 31; Keystone Collection, p. 55; Paris Match, M. Courriere, cover; Popperfoto, p. 50; Topham Picture Library, p. 15.

Map drawn by Geoffrey Pleasance

Exley Publications would particularly like to thank Mrs. Vreni Mark, director of the Albert Schweitzer Archive in Günsbach, and Dr. Kathleen Collins, Archivist of the Albert Schweitzer Center in Massachusetts, for their invaluable help in obtaining pictures for this book and for additional information about Dr. Schweitzer in later years.

North American edition first published in 1989 by
Gareth Stevens, Inc.
7317 West Green Tree Road
Milwaukee, WI 53223 USA

First published in the United Kingdom in 1988
with an original text © by James Bentley.
Additional end matter © 1989 by Gareth Stevens Inc.

Library of Congress Cataloging-in-Publication Data

Bentley, James, 1937-
    Albert Schweitzer / by James Bentley.
        p. cm.--(People who have helped the world)
    Includes index.
    Summary: Examines the life of the humanitarian who pursued medical missionary work in the jungles of Africa while developing his spiritual beliefs about the value of all life.
    ISBN 1-55532-823-7   (lib. bdg.)
    1. Schweitzer, Albert, 1875-1965--Juvenile literature. 2. Missionaries, Medical--Gabon-- Biography--Juvenile literature. 3. Theologians--Europe--Biography--Juvenile literature. 4. Musicians--Europe--Biography--Juvenile literature. 5. Gabon--Biography--Juvenile literature. 6. Europe--Biography--Juvenile literature. [1. Schweitzer, Albert, 1875-1965. 2. Missionaries. 3. Physicians.]
    I. Title. II. Series.
    CT1018.S45B45   1988
    610'.92'4--dc19
    [B]
    [92]   88-17731

Series conceived and edited by Helen Exley
Picture research: Kate Duffy
Research: Diana Briscoe
Editorial: Gail Jarrett and Margaret Montgomery
Series editor, U.S.: Rhoda Irene Sherwood
Editorial assistant, U.S.: Scott Enk

Printed in Hungary

1 2 3 4 5 6 7 8 9 94 93 92 91 90 89

ALBERT SCHWEITZER

The doctor who gave up a
brilliant career to serve
the people of Africa

by James Bentley

Gareth Stevens Publishing
Milwaukee

A hospital in the jungle

It is 1913, and a German doctor is operating on black patients at a place called Lambaréné, in the African jungle. His hospital is a tiny room in a converted chicken coop. His trusted black assistant, Joseph Avzawami, sterilizes the doctor's instruments by plunging them into boiling water. Then he hands them through the door into the tiny operating room. The doctor's wife gives the patients the anesthetic that puts them to sleep. Then Joseph puts on long rubber gloves and comes in to help. Outside, the relatives of the patients sit on the ground, feeding themselves and patiently hoping that their loved ones may be cured by this strange white man who can put them to sleep, cut them open, remove a part of their bodies, sew them up again, and return them to life.

This doctor was to become one of the most famous men of the twentieth century. Not yet forty years old, he had already made a name for himself as a world-famous musician, religious thinker, and writer. His name was Albert Schweitzer.

Hideous diseases

We know what he thought about his mission and what he meant to these patients who were suffering terrible, crippling diseases. He was their last hope. He once wrote about his first major surgical operation in Africa: "When the poor moaning creature came, I laid my hand on his forehead and said, 'Don't be afraid. You will go to sleep, and when you wake up you will feel no more pain.'"

The most common illnesses Schweitzer came across in Africa were skin diseases, malaria, leprosy, sleeping sickness, tropical dysentery, ulcers, and hernias.

"Schweitzer. He is one of the personalities of this century who has become almost a myth. His sacrificial work in Africa, the natural outlet for his vital, practical philosophy of life, established him as a saint in the minds of millions. His compassion for the animal kingdom, his creation of a jungle hospital, his plea for international understanding amid a global arms race — all seemed to set him apart from common humanity."
From Schweitzer: A Biography, *by George Marshall and David Poling*

Opposite: Albert Schweitzer returning to his beloved hospital in Gabon, Africa, from a fund-raising visit to Europe. Decades earlier Schweitzer had read about the desperate suffering of the people of Africa. He had decided to do anything, to give the rest of his life, to help. He devoted the next fifty years working to build his jungle hospital at Lambaréné.

5

When a hernia broke through a membrane, unless Schweitzer and his team operated promptly, the sufferer would die in intense pain. Frequently, too, Schweitzer was faced with horrible wounds from snake bites and attacks from wild animals that roamed the jungle.

Sometimes the patients themselves would undermine his work. They might bathe in the filthy Ogowé River the day after an operation — unconcerned that their dressings became wet and dirty. Or they might eat a large meal after a serious stomach operation. Or they might insert a grubby finger under a dressing to feel the wound. Schweitzer did his best to stop these habits. Relatives of patients turned out to be a different problem — they would come to comfort patients but would get into hospital beds late at night. The sick person might end up sleeping on the floor.

Albert Schweitzer's patients

As Schweitzer's fame grew throughout the jungle, patients came from two hundred miles up or down the Ogowé River. More and more patients began walking huge distances for operations. They would often arrive at the hospital half-starved and exhausted. The doctor and his staff would then have to nurse them for several weeks just so the patients could become healthy enough to be operated on.

These native peoples saw the jungle hospital as their only hope. Within the first nine months, Albert Schweitzer had treated nearly seven thousand patients. By the late 1940s, around five thousand a year were arriving for treatment — men, women, and children paddling in dugout canoes along the river or simply walking to the hospital at Lambaréné.

These patients knew precisely what they wanted from the great jungle doctor. One popular story shows just how clear they were about their needs: One of Schweitzer's surgeons decided to cheer up a patient before the operation. He began chatting in a friendly way as she lay on the operating table waiting for the anesthetic. She paid no attention. He continued chatting. Finally, she interrupted him, saying, "This is no time for gossip. You should cut."

His books and his music

Albert Schweitzer ran this jungle hospital for the rest of his long life — more than fifty years. These years were interrupted by gaps totaling about seven years. The gaps were caused mainly by World War I and its aftermath, and health and financial problems for Schweitzer and his wife.

During those many years in Africa, many people came to regard him as a saint. By day, he operated on his patients. By night, he wrote both profound books and simple books that were read by millions of men and women. One of these works, *The Philosophy of Civilization*, appeared in 1923 and sold half a million copies. In between writing books and performing operations, he played a piano specially constructed with organ pedals and made to withstand the extremes of the jungle climate.

Some people disliked this great man — perhaps because they envied him, or perhaps because they

Patients at Schweitzer's first jungle hospital, sitting in the open air and waiting to be treated. Diseases such as dysentery, malaria, sleeping sickness, leprosy, and elephantiasis were all common. Patients were treated free, although those who could afford it often paid with a chicken, an egg, or some other food.

7

The hospital at Lambaréné was an informal place, with children wandering around happily and patients sitting outside wherever they wished. It was always overcrowded, while the large, white European-style hospitals had few patients.

misunderstood him. The chicken-coop hospital was replaced by a better one, built by the doctor himself and his black friends. But some critics complained because Schweitzer's jungle hospital was not equipped with every piece of modern equipment.

Answering his critics

But Schweitzer knew how to defend himself. In those days the part of Africa where he worked was primitive. Many other white doctors had no patients — the African people still relied on witch doctors with charms, fetishes, and remedies taken from nature. If he were to get the Africans to come to his hospital, it couldn't be too strange to them.

Schweitzer wondered how people who knew nothing about Africa could tell him how to run an African hospital. At first, he confessed, he too had wanted to build a hospital like the ones in Europe, but two local workmen showed him that he was wrong. His was to be a hospital to suit African tastes, not European.

The hospital was more of an African village attached to a clinic than a modern hospital with a forbidding white building, strange beds, and machines. There were no wards, but long bungalows with cubicles. Most patients were surrounded and cared for by their families, who shared a cubicle. There was no electricity except in the operating room, so the Africans cooked on smoky burners. The ground was rough, with no paved areas. Animals wandered around freely. This felt like home to the local people but horrified many overseas visitors.

Schweitzer's African hospital worked. It grew to more than seventy buildings serving an astonishing six hundred patients a day. Over the years, more than seventy devoted nurses and doctors from as far away as Japan, France, and the United States were inspired to follow Dr. Schweitzer into the African jungle to work at his hospital. But because the hospital was so popular with patients, the medical team was always understaffed. In 1965, the year Schweitzer died, there were only six doctors and thirty-five nurses looking after six hundred patients. Between Schweitzer's arrival in Africa and his death, he and his co-workers had treated over one-and-a-half million sick Africans and performed nearly twenty thousand operations. They set up a separate village large enough to hold 180 people suffering from the dreaded disease, leprosy.

"He had a real understanding of when a man was sick, these critical moments in a doctor's career when he must decide to hold off treatment sometimes. When he was just causing the man more misery he would instinctively feel it. He could tell when a man was near death. . . . I can remember him ordering me to incise a big abscess sometimes when I thought I'd just wait another day. He'd say: 'No, now, today, this minute, you must incise it today, no more delay.' And he was right, every time. There would be a pint or two of pus in this man's leg — these big tropical abscesses."
Dr. Frank Catchpool

Africa changes

By 1965 the Africa served by his hospital at Lambaréné had changed dramatically. No longer a French colony, it had become the Republic of Gabon. But Schweitzer's original vision was as appropriate as it had been in the beginning. When Schweitzer died, the president of Gabon showed Schweitzer had been right to resist having a European-style hospital in Africa. The president begged the hospital's chief surgeon and Rhena, Schweitzer's daughter, to keep the old buildings Schweitzer had supervised. Inside the hospital, the president insisted, his people felt at home.

Black Africa paid Schweitzer another great compliment. In 1959 the United Nations asked the government of Gabon to send a representative to the UN Commission on Human Rights. Schweitzer was asked to go. "Impossible," he wrote back on the invitation itself. "My hospital needs me."

Schweitzer becomes famous

People from other nations recognized the value of his work and respected his dedication. A Frenchman, Jacques Feschotte, met Schweitzer after World War II. The whole day, Feschotte said, was like a miracle: "I could hardly speak: my heart was beating too fast." Schweitzer, he judged, "has enough knowledge, and enough moral strength, for a dozen exceptional men; and he moves as easily among the practical arrangements of everyday life as among the eternal problems of religion and philosophy."

In 1947, *Life* magazine described Schweitzer as the greatest man in the world. The brilliant scientist Albert Einstein wrote to him a year later, "You are one of the few who combine extraordinary energy and many-sidedness with the desire to serve man and to lighten his lot."

In 1955, when Schweitzer was almost eighty, Dr. Howard A. Rusk wrote in *The New York Times* that "few men in history have equalled his achievements." Schweitzer, he said, was supreme "as a theologian interpreting the works of Jesus, a musician interpreting the works of Bach, a scholar interpreting the writings of Goethe, a philosopher interpreting history, and a missionary bringing healing and understanding to French Equatorial Africa."

Childhood in Alsace

Yet like many people who succeed in later life, as a child, Albert Schweitzer had hated his first day at school. He later remarked: "When on a fine October day my father for the first time put a slate under my arm and led me away to the school-mistress, I cried the whole way there." Until then he had wandered free around the hills and valleys of the Münster

Albert Schweitzer's father, Pastor Louis, bearded, stern, yet kindly. He first taught Albert to love music and the Bible.

valley, sometimes playing with friends, at other times preferring to be alone.

Albert Schweitzer was born on January 14, 1875, in Kaysersberg, a lovely town in Alsace on the border between France and Germany. Kaysersberg is washed by the Weiss River, and the river is spanned by an ancient bridge built in 1511, with a little chapel in the middle. Vineyards rise on the gentle slopes outside the town. A ruined castle looms over the place. And of the walls that once protected Kaysersberg from raiders, four massive towers still stand. Though today Alsace is French, in 1875 it belonged to Germany, so Albert Schweitzer was born a German.

By the time he was six months old, his parents had moved to another village about fifteen miles (twenty-four km) away. Albert's father, Louis, was a Protestant clergyman. He was offered the position of pastor at the church of Günsbach, a village in the Münster valley. Günsbach is not as beautiful as Kaysersberg, but little Albert grew to adore the place. It lies on the Fecht River, surrounded by gentle rolling hills, and is not far from the mountains.

In 1928, when Schweitzer was fifty-three, he was awarded the Goethe Prize for "his general services to humanity." He used the prize money to build a home for himself in Günsbach. Today it is a Schweitzer museum, filled with copies of nearly all his letters as well as the little crib he rocked in as a baby, his books, his pianos and organs, many photographs, and the manuscripts of the books he wrote.

Schweitzer's mother, Adéle Schillinger, who was tragically trampled to death by German cavalry in World War I.

Albert at school

The boy who cried all the way to school on his first day did no better when he got there. He preferred to look out the window, dreaming, rather than to learn how to read and write. His mother cried over his poor grades. But in later years, Schweitzer was to write many books that would change the world.

Throughout his whole life, Albert Schweitzer also loved music. His father taught him to play the church organ, and he was only nine years old when he first sat in for the organist at his father's Günsbach church. Soon the gifted child was working out music of his

own. "I did not play much from notes," he remembered. "My delight was to improvise, and to reproduce songs and hymn tunes with an accompaniment of my own invention."

When he went to school he was surprised to find that the music teacher simply played tunes with one finger, adding not the slightest accompaniment. Albert asked why she did not play them "properly," with harmony. Then he sat down and skillfully played a hymn, adding a four-part harmony. To her credit, the teacher from then on became his friend, even though she continued to pick out a tune herself with one finger. For the first time it occurred to Albert that he could do something she could not. He became confused and was ashamed that he'd shown off this

> *"I did not look forward to going to school. When on a fine October day my father for the first time put a slate under my arm and led me away to the schoolmistress, I cried the whole way there, for I suspected that an end had now come to my dreams and my glorious freedom."*
>
> *Albert Schweitzer*

*The village of Günsbach
in Alsace, France, with
the church where
Schweitzer's father
was pastor and where
Schweitzer first learned
to play the organ.*

alarming knowledge. He pretended to her that he was
really not so bright.

Wrestling with other boys

Albert was a sensitive boy. Even as a child, he showed
the compassion that would fuel his deeds as an adult.
He was troubled by the fact that some of the children
in the village of Günsbach were much poorer than he
was. One day he wrestled with a bigger boy named
George Nitschelm. George should have won, but
Albert beat him. George Nitschelm was a bad loser,
and he cried out, "If I got broth to eat twice a week, as
you do, I'd be as strong as you." Albert was cut to the
heart so much so that soon he began to hate the soup
that his mother served him.

Albert also loathed wearing clothes that set him apart from the other village boys. They didn't wear overcoats, so he wouldn't wear one. They wore clogs instead of shoes, so he gave up his shoes.

One day his mother took him to Strasbourg to buy him a new cap. The clerk in the shop brought out a fine sailor's cap, but because no other boy in Günsbach wore such a cap, Albert angrily refused to put it on. The clerk became annoyed with him, asking impatiently, "What kind of hat *do* you want?" Albert replied that he wanted one like those the village boys wore. When no such cap could be found in the shop, Albert's mother insisted that the clerk send for one. She did not particularly like that sort of hat, but she understood that it was important to Albert.

From an early age, Albert sided with anyone who was hurt or badly treated. His fellow schoolboys used

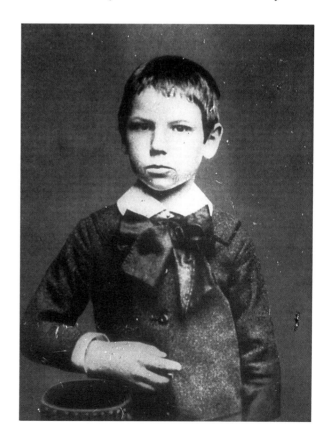

Young Albert Schweitzer, aged seven, and looking quite serious.

14

to make fun of a man named Mausche, a Jewish cattle and land dealer who would ride in from a nearby village on his donkey cart. Mausche was the only Jew anyone in Günsbach had ever seen, and the Günsbach boys would run after his cart, making fun of him and crying "Mausche, Mausche." Albert watched the man drive out of the village without apparently caring about these insults.

From time to time Mausche even turned around and smiled at them all. "This smile overpowered me," Albert Schweitzer remembered. From then on he refused to run behind the donkey cart with the rest of the Günsbach boys. Instead he would politely welcome Mausche and shake hands with him before walking alongside his cart.

Hatred of violence and suffering

Soon Albert began to hate every kind of violence. In his young days, he'd hated fighting against weaker children. But when he was nine or ten, he was playing a game against his sister Adéle. She was so bad at it that Albert angrily struck her in the face. Albert then realized that he, too, could be more violent than anyone ought to be. Shocked by his own violence, Schweitzer gradually gave up all games. He decided that his immense desire to win was wrong.

Not surprisingly, this tormented child was miserable when others were suffering — even animals. It was to become the whole basis of the older Albert Schweitzer's way of looking at the world. "So far back as I can remember I was saddened by the amount of misery I saw in the world around me," Schweitzer recalled of his childhood. "One thing that specially saddened me was that the unfortunate animals had to suffer so much pain and misery. The sight of an old limping horse, tugged forward by one man while another kept beating it with a stick to get it to the knacker's yard at Colmar, haunted me for weeks."

Once, he saw a dog attacking a neighbor's horse. Albert only wanted to frighten off the dog with a flick of his whip, but his whip hit the dog in the eye. Horrified, Albert began asking God to "protect and bless *all* living creatures" in his bedtime prayers.

Albert Schweitzer was born in Kayserberg, in the Alsace. This region, lying between France and Germany, has over the centuries belonged to each in turn. In 1871, after the Franco-Prussian War, it had become part of Germany. It became part of France again in 1918, when Albert was 43.

"Thou shalt not kill"

This simple prayer brought problems to Albert, for his days spent with other children involved innocent hunting. One spring day, when Schweitzer was scarcely eight years old, a friend suggested they shoot some birds. Albert didn't want to, but he agreed. Like many young people, he suspected his friend would laugh at him if he refused. So the two boys armed themselves with slingshots and set out. The leaves had barely returned to the trees, so the birds were clearly visible to them and quite defenseless. His friend took aim. So did Albert. At just that moment, the church bells began to ring. Albert, remembering his prayer, shooed the birds away.

From that day on, whenever church bells rang out, he gratefully remembered how on that day the bells had driven deep into his heart the rule, "Thou shalt not kill." Albert felt so strongly that he must not kill or torture his fellow creatures that it no longer mattered what the other children thought.

And this was a second lesson for Albert. As he put it, he began to "unlearn" his dread of being laughed at by his friends. He began to realize that he might be more sensitive than his friends to certain things, and this was going to set him apart from them. He had to harden himself so that he did not go against his own beliefs just to win their good opinion.

This was the starting point of Schweitzer's later belief in what he called "reverence for life." He found himself disagreeing with his friends about harming animals. Twice, other boys persuaded him to go fishing. But Albert found he could not tolerate the simple act of sticking the hooks into the worms that were used for bait. It revolted him. So did wrenching open the mouths of fish he caught. Schweitzer was so affected by this that he even tried to stop other boys from going fishing.

Instead, he found a new pleasure in the countryside. When he was nine, he went to a new school two miles (three km) away from Günsbach. Because there was no transportation, he had to walk there and back. He loved it, and for the rest of his life he adored the countryside around Günsbach.

"So far back as I can remember I was saddened by the amount of misery I saw in the world around me. One thing that specially saddened me was that the unfortunate animals had to suffer so much pain and misery. The sight of an old limping horse, tugged forward by one man while another kept beating it with a stick to get it to the knacker's yard at Colmar, haunted me for weeks."

Albert Schweitzer

16

The church at Günsbach

He also loved his father's church in Günsbach. There he learned that people of different beliefs could live happily at peace with each other. Alsace had suffered terribly as a battleground — especially during the religious wars of the sixteenth century and during the Thirty Years' War in the seventeenth century. In both conflicts, Catholics and Protestants had slaughtered each other. Their miseries were made worse by famine and plague. Nowhere did these conflicts rage more fiercely than in the land of Albert Schweitzer's birth, the midpoint between Protestant Germany and Catholic France.

As a result, a degree of religious tolerance that was found scarcely anywhere else in the world existed in Alsace. Protestants and Catholics agreed to share the same churches. At Günsbach the Catholics worshipped in the east end of the village church, the part known as the chancel.

To Albert's youthful gaze the Catholic chancel of the Günsbach church was magnificent. There was an altar painted to look like gold, with huge branches of artificial flowers upon it, and tall metal candlesticks with majestic wax candles in them. On the wall, above the altar and between the two windows, were two large gilded statues of St. Joseph and the Virgin Mary. All these objects were flooded in light.

Schweitzer also found here a deep satisfaction in the way in which two separate religious communities could live so close together and yet so peacefully. As he later wrote: "When I was still only a child I felt it to be a beautiful thing that in our village Catholics and Protestants worshipped in the same building."

Secondary school

Although Albert's parents had more money than the other villagers in Günsbach, they were still poor — feeding and clothing another four children as well as Albert. They knew that Albert needed the best possible education, because he was obviously extremely bright. But they could not afford to send him to one of the best schools in Germany.

"All my life I have been glad that I began in the village school. It was a good thing for me that in the process of learning I had to measure myself with the village boys, and thus make it quite clear to myself that they had at least as much in their heads as I had in mine."
Albert Schweitzer

Albert at the age of nine, with a fine watch chain. Always a shy person, he looks anxiously at the camera.

17

From the Schweitzer family album. Albert, aged seventeen, sits on the left. Next to him are his brother, Pauli, his sister Margrit, one of their friends, and his two other sisters, Adéle and Louise.

The answer to their problem came from Albert's Great-uncle Louis, who lived with his wife, Sophie, at a town called Mülhausen, where they ran the elementary school. He and Great-aunt Sophie would look after him for nothing. The school was obviously a great deal better than the local village schools, so in 1885, when Albert was ten, he was sent to Mülhausen.

At first he hated it. No longer could he wander alone among the hills and up the mountains around Günsbach. "I felt as if I were being torn away from Nature," he wrote. Later on he realized how generous Great-uncle Louis and Great-aunt Sophie had been. "Had it not been for their kindness," he later admitted, "my father, who had nothing beyond his slender wage on which to bring up his large family, could hardly have afforded to send me to such a fine school."

Great-aunt Sophie sometimes sensed how much he missed the countryside of Günsbach. One sunny March day when she was ironing, she saw him looking moodily out of the window at the last melting snows on the mountains. To his delight she said, "It's too fine a day to spend indoors." She asked if he would like to go for a walk. So they walked over the canal, which still bore blocks of ice, and up the mountainside. From then on Albert appreciated his great-aunt even more, for she understood his deepest longings.

By this time Albert had begun to love reading. He used to skim through a book in bed because he could not bear to put it down before he had reached the end. Sometimes he sat up all night to finish a long one.

At the age of fourteen, the shy Albert Schweitzer suddenly found his voice. For the next two years, the noise the boy made upset everyone. His passion for talking annoyed even his father, who liked conversation. "I emerged from the shell of reserve in which up till now I had hidden myself and became the one who disrupted every pleasant conversation," Albert remembered. His great-aunt scolded him for arguing with adults as if they were his own age.

Playing the piano and organ

Albert had started playing the piano when he was about five, but now his great-uncle and great-aunt insisted that he play regularly. At first the strict routine was hard for Albert. He was forced to play after lunch until school started again. If he finished his homework early in the evening, then he was back on the piano. But soon Great-uncle Louis found him a teacher, a brilliant organist named Eugen Münch. Eugen Münch had just arrived from the Berlin music high school to take up the post of organist at the church of St. Stephen in tiny Mülhausen.

At first he could scarcely bear teaching Schweitzer, his shy pupil. Albert was "a thorn in the flesh," he shouted. Two problems were coming between them. One was that Albert was dreamily making up his own music on his great-aunt's piano instead of properly

"Joy, sorrow, tears, lamentations, laughter — to all these music gives voice, but in such a way that we are transported from the world of unrest to the world of peace, and see reality in a new way, as if we were sitting by a mountain lake and contemplating hills and woods and clouds in the tranquil and fathomless water."
Albert Schweitzer

This powerful statue of a black man by the sculptor Frédéric Auguste Bartholdi made a deep and lasting impression on the young Albert Schweitzer. "His face, with its sad, thoughtful expression, spoke to me of the misery of the dark continent," he wrote. Later he would declare that "if a record could be made of all that has happened between the white and colored races, some of the pages . . . would be turned over unread, because their contents would be too horrible for the reader."

learning the pieces Münch gave him. The other problem was that Albert was afraid of showing Münch all he was capable of playing.

One day Eugen Münch became really angry, for Albert had just played a sonata by Mozart that the teenager had hardly practiced. Münch opened a copy of one of the German composer Felix Mendelssohn's *Songs Without Words*, with the words, "Really you don't deserve to have such beautiful music given you to play. You'll come and spoil this 'Lied Ohne Worte' for me, just like everything else." Eugen Münch ended these remarks with the insult, "If a boy has no feeling, I certainly can't give him any."

An inspired teacher

The brilliant teacher's anger stirred Albert. His sensitive pride was wounded, and he now had to defend — and prove — himself. Throughout the following two weeks he played the piece again and again. Although no one had yet taught him how to use his fingers properly, he found the best fingers to use for each note, making notes above the music. When his next lesson with Münch took place, Schweitzer patiently sat through the exercises with his fingers and with scales. Then he braced himself and played the same piece from Mendelssohn's *Songs Without Words* from the depths of his soul.

At the end, Eugen Münch hardly spoke. Placing his hands firmly on Albert's shoulders, he moved the boy from the piano. Münch sat down himself and played another of Mendelssohn's *Songs Without Words* that Albert had never heard. The music entranced the boy.

Münch was so impressed by Albert's talent that he allowed him to have lessons on the church organ. When he was sixteen, Albert took Münch's place playing the organ at church services in Mülhausen. He would eventually become a famous musician.

Not long after, Albert was trusted by his great teacher to play the organ accompaniment to another splendid piece of music, Brahms's *Requiem,* sung by the choir of the village church, St. Stephen's. He later wrote, "Then, for the first time, I knew the joy, which I have so often tasted since then, of letting the organ send the flood of its own special tones to mingle with the clanging music of the choir and orchestra."

Albert questions the Bible

From childhood on, Albert was equally fascinated with religion, especially with the Bible. He was inspired by what he read. But soon he stopped believing that everything he read in the Bible was true. Some things he read seemed wonderful. Others were puzzling. As one of the world's most famous religious thinkers, he would later write: "Reason, I said to myself, is given us that we may bring everything within the range of its action, even the most exalted ideas of religion." In the Bible, he would always find things that he found perplexing. The young boy and the more mature teenager began to question everything in the Old and New Testaments, though still wanting to know more about the greatest subjects of the Bible — God and Jesus.

In his first year at school, Albert had questioned his father about the great flood described in the Old

Colmar, where Bartholdi's statue stood, was for Albert Schweitzer a glimpse of a fascinating world outside his own village — a world of dancing and parks, of bands and boats, of bicycles and museums, of exquisite houses and pretty girls.

Testament. The Old Testament declared that after forty days and forty nights of rain the whole world had been covered with water. That summer in Alsace was a wet one. He asked his father why, since it had rained for nearly forty days and forty nights, the tops of the Günsbach houses, let alone the peaks of the Vosges Mountains, had not been covered with water, as described in the Biblical story. Pastor Louis answered his small son: "At that time, at the beginning of the world it didn't rain just in drops, but like pouring water out of buckets."

Later, when one of Albert's teachers told her class the story of the flood, Schweitzer was astonished that she didn't mention the buckets. He scolded from his seat, "Teacher, you must tell the story correctly."

At another time, when reading the New Testament, Albert became fascinated by the story of three kings who brought gold and other valuable presents to baby Jesus. He understood that Jesus, Mary, and Joseph had been poor. "Why?" he asked himself. "What did the parents of Jesus do . . . with the gold and other valuables which they got from these men? How could they have been poor after that?" Why didn't these so-called wise men trouble themselves again about Jesus? Why didn't they look in on him again?

School examinations

In time, Albert began to enjoy his studies and to learn. At first, he had shown little promise at Mülhausen. But a change of teachers brought a change of attitude, and Albert was to become a brilliant pupil. His best subject was history and he enjoyed science, but languages and mathematics remained difficult for him. He discovered that he loved poetry — sometimes he would hide away and read poems when he should have been studying something else. He would defend himself by saying that when he was reading poetry he had to shut the shop windows in order to keep out the noise in the streets.

In 1893, at age eighteen, Albert took his final secondary school exams. Although he was nervous about how well he would do, he passed with ease and was given a place at the University of Strasbourg.

Music versus religion

Schweitzer had to decide whether to study music or religion. This was not going to be an easy choice, for he loved music just as much as he respected the Bible and the church. Schweitzer confessed, "Between the ages of sixteen and eighteen I found battling within myself a dispute over whether my calling should be in the field of music or of religion." The charms of music drew him powerfully. "I long to become organist of a beautiful church," he said.

One composer revered in Europe in those days was Richard Wagner. When he was sixteen, Schweitzer heard a performance of Wagner's opera *Tannhäuser.* "This music overpowered me to so great an extent that days passed before I was able to start properly concentrating on my lessons again," he recalled.

Yet he also thought he would like to work with people and encourage them to worship God and obey the commands of Jesus. Finally, Schweitzer chose to study religion and philosophy. But in the gap between leaving school and beginning his university years in Strasbourg he indulged his other passionate calling by spending some time in Paris, where he studied music. There he met a superb organist who became his teacher and his friend.

This man was Charles-Marie Widor, the famous organist at the church of St. Sulpice in Paris. He also taught organ lessons and had the pick of the organ students of western Europe.

Into his presence came the shy Albert Schweitzer. But on the way to his first interview with the great man, Albert was held up by a Paris traffic jam. When he finally arrived, late for his appointment, Widor was waiting impatiently. He asked Schweitzer what he wished to play. Albert answered, "Bach, of course."

No answer could have been better. Widor, who loved the organ music of Johann Sebastian Bach, listened to the performance of Eugen Münch's pupil. Listening to Schweitzer prompted him to break a life-long rule of caution — he instantly accepted Albert Schweitzer as his pupil. These two men were to become fast friends. Later, Albert would often return to Paris to study with Widor.

"Schweitzer came to survey his happiness and to wonder if it was right for him to accept it unthinkingly. On the one hand there were the warmth and tenderness of his family life, the satisfaction of work well done, the knowledge that the joys of music would grow ever more intense. And on the other, the pain and suffering of the world."

Jacques Feschotte, one of Schweitzer's close friends

Schweitzer at the organ of St. Nicholas Church, Strasbourg. Music would be a lifelong source of personal strength. "Music gives voice to joy and sorrow, tears and laughter," he wrote, "but in such a way that it takes us from a world of unrest to a world of peace."

Schweitzer, already a famous writer at the age of thirty-one and sporting an elegant boater hat and a cane.

"The decision was made when I was one and twenty. In that year, while still a student, I resolved to devote my life till I was thirty to the office of preacher, to science and to music. If by that time I should have done what I hoped in science and music, I would take a path of immediate service as a man to my fellow men."

Albert Schweitzer

Albert goes to the university

At the end of October 1893, Schweitzer went to Strasbourg. At the time, it was the most liberal university in Europe. Students were encouraged to work independently and to make their own judgments. It was this atmosphere that encouraged Albert to question the meaning of life and religion. Albert himself boasted, when he reached the university as a student, "Strassburg University was then at the height of its reputation. Unhampered by tradition, teachers and students alike strove to realize the ideal of a modern University. There were hardly any professors of advanced age on the teaching staff. A fresh breeze of youthfulness penetrated everywhere."

In the middle of his course, he had to serve for a year in the army. But Albert didn't mind; when he went on training exercises, he took a Greek New Testament with him. He would sit in the army tent and in trenches reading happily. His commanding officer, who became his friend, allowed Albert to attend any important lectures at the university.

Albert made rapid progress at Strasbourg. The years passed quickly. His teachers recognized his talents and persuaded Albert that he must now become a doctor of philosophy. His studies took him to universities in Paris and Berlin, where he encountered some of the finest minds of the time.

Then in 1899, at the age of twenty-four, he returned to Strasbourg to take his doctorate in philosophy. His teachers wanted him to pursue further studies in philosophy, but this would have clashed with Albert's wish to be a preacher. "To me," Albert wrote, "preaching was a necessity of my being." So Albert completed his doctorate and continued with theology.

The young university lecturer

Even though his days as a full-time student were over, Albert remained in Strasbourg. On December 1, 1899, he took up the position of preacher at the Church of St. Nicholas in Strasbourg.

Albert could still be shy. And in spite of his brilliance, he was also humble. Once, some members of the congregation at St. Nicholas complained that his sermons were too short. Albert defended himself by saying that he was "only a poor curate who stopped speaking when [he] had nothing more to say."

During this period, Albert continued his studies in theology, and in 1900, he was awarded a licentiate in theology, a degree just below the doctorate.

He became Principal of Strasbourg's Theological College of St. Thomas, where he gained the respect of all who encountered him. Part of the immense reputation he was to make came from the fact that at this time he had boundless energy. He never seemed to stop working — as a musician, as a university teacher, as a writer. Charles Münch, conductor of the Boston Symphony Orchestra, observed that "Schweitzer's capacity for work is incredible. I have often seen him, after a full and strenuous day of activity, sit down with students and take the time to correct their work and to guide them through new problems. His talents and abilities are manifold."

The young Albert had learned to work hard when he was just a child. One day, he came home from school with a bad report. His grandmother wept. "I couldn't bear to see her cry," Schweitzer remembered. "I took her head in my hands and kissed her and promised to work. It was then that I realized I loved her more than I could tell. I've kept my promise."

"When one considers that, by the time he was twenty, Schweitzer was fluent in Greek, Latin, Hebrew, German and French; that he was recognized as one of the most brilliant students at the University of Strassburg; that he wrote his doctoral dissertation based on one of the most difficult of all philosophers to understand; that by the time he was twenty-seven he was a professor himself and one of the greatest concert organists in Europe, one gains some understanding of the man's extraordinary qualities."

from Portraits of Nobel Laureates in Peace

The scholar and organ builder

The once-anxious schoolboy was rapidly becoming a famous scholar — in the world of music as well as religion. When he was thirty, Schweitzer helped start the Paris Bach Society. He would spend a part of each of the next eight years in Paris, playing the organ to accompany the society's concerts. He loved this work. "I have a passion for music," he used to say, "the way other people have a passion for wine or tobacco."

Soon Albert Schweitzer became well known for his new understanding of the organ music of Johann Sebastian Bach. Schweitzer had adored Bach's music from his early youth. He would visit Widor, the French organist, in Paris for several weeks each spring, working with him on the manuscripts of the musician they both loved. When a New York publisher asked Widor to prepare an edition of Bach's complete organ works, Widor insisted that Schweitzer help him with the work. The publisher agreed and eventually eight volumes of *The Complete Organ Works of J. S. Bach* appeared. Because Widor died in 1937, before the work was finished, only the first five were by Schweitzer and Widor.

Soon Schweitzer was playing Bach's organ works on every great organ in Europe. But eventually he became dissatisfied with the organs he played on. In his view they were not fit to convey the excitement of Bach's music. So Schweitzer decided that he would become an organ builder. In time, his rebuilt organs became as famous as his own musical performances.

Schweitzer's views on Christ

At the same time, Schweitzer was working out his views about Jesus Christ. His conclusions were controversial. Schweitzer believed Christ had made one tragic mistake. Christ, he wrote, believed that if he sacrificed himself, if he did not fight back against those who hurt him, if he turned the other cheek instead — the world would become a better place. Instead, Christ was simply executed, and people did not change at all. Instead, as Schweitzer put it, "The world is full of suffering."

Schweitzer experienced this suffering in his own spirit. Only rarely, he confessed, did he feel glad to be alive. So it makes sense that Schweitzer would be drawn to the Christ who denied the world and deliberately accepted suffering. As a child, Schweitzer possessed tragic traits that made it almost inevitable for him to model himself on this noble, tragic Jesus.

To share the burdens of others

Opposite: The scholar at the peak of his powers, conscious that he had gifts in music, religion, and philosophy that few people could match.

Inside Albert Schweitzer was in deep torment. He was already a famous man, yet he felt that he was not sharing in the life of Jesus, whom he deeply respected. Above all, he believed that he must try to make the world a little less miserable, even if it meant that he himself should suffer in this aim.

"It seemed to me a matter of course that we should all take a share of the burden of pain that lies upon the world," he wrote. The world is ultimately miserable, Schweitzer believed, although few wished to accept this fact. He remembered, "Even while I was a boy at school it was clear to me that no explanation of the evil in the world could ever satisfy me. All explanations, I felt, ended in silly excuses and at bottom had no other object than to make it possible for people to experience the misery around them without really feeling it."

Schweitzer decided he would not just experience this misery. He would do what he could to ease the world's suffering.

For him, the essential element of the preaching of Jesus was that "only through love can we attain communion with God." He became convinced that it was "horrible" to cause suffering and death. He grew more and more certain that at the bottom of our hearts, every one of us feels this, but we fail to acknowledge it in case other people laugh at us. Our best sentiments become blunted. "I vowed that I would never let my feelings get blunted," Schweitzer wrote.

Schweitzer decides to train as a doctor

Schweitzer now saw that for him concern for others demanded practical activity on their behalf. He had already worked among neglected children and in the past had helped men who were tramps or homeless. He wanted to do more. He enjoyed his life as a preacher and teacher. But instead of talking about the religion of love, he felt he must put it into practice.

This desire would lead him to the African jungle.

As a child he had been deeply moved by a statue in the town of Colmar, not far from Günsbach. The sculptor was Frédéric Auguste Bartholdi, who had become famous for designing the Statue of Liberty. What touched Schweitzer was a statue of a brooding, melancholy, powerful African man. Bartholdi had put into this statue his own understanding of all the sufferings black people had endured at the hands of whites. Schweitzer gazed at the statue and felt he understood that suffering.

A man suffering from the dreaded disease leprosy. Unless leprosy is treated in time, the sufferer's fingers and toes drop off, and white patches and huge ugly sores appear on the person's skin. The result is grotesque disfiguration. At Lambaréné, Schweitzer set up a separate leper hospital to treat victims of the disease.

The needs of the Congo mission

One day, in the autumn of 1904, Albert opened the latest issue of the journal of the Missionary Society of Paris. Inside was an article by its president, Dr. Alfred Boegner, on "The needs of the Congo Mission." In those days the Upper Congo was part of the French Empire, and was called French Equatorial Africa. Today it belongs to the Republic of Gabon. Alfred Boegner wrote of the horrible diseases of that region. African men, women, and children desperately needed doctors. Boegner appealed to Christians to offer themselves for this work.

Albert knew at once this was what he wanted to do. His search for a way to serve his fellow human beings was over. He decided to become a missionary doctor in Africa. "Medical knowledge," he later wrote, "made it possible for me to carry out my intention in the best and most complete way, wherever the path of service might lead me."

The following January he announced to his congregation at St. Nicholas Church that Christians had to make amends — "atonement," he called it, for all the wrongs done to black men and women. "We must make atonement for all the terrible crimes we read of in the newspapers. We must make atonement for the still worse ones which we do not read about in the newspapers, crimes that are shrouded in the silence of the jungle night."

But Albert Schweitzer was a musician and religious genius, not a doctor. So he resigned from all his university posts and at the age of thirty registered as a medical student.

His family and friends tried to stop him. Conditions in that part of Africa were dangerous, they argued, and Schweitzer had a great future before him in Europe. But Albert wouldn't be put off. In October 1905, he began his medical training, which would last for the next seven years.

Schweitzer finds a wife

During this period Albert met his wife. She was Hélène Bresslau, daughter of Harry Bresslau, head of

The woman Schweitzer was to marry, Hélène Bresslau. She trained as a nurse to help Albert in his work before they set off together for French Equatorial Africa to start their hospital.

the history department at the University of Strasbourg. He and Albert Schweitzer had been great friends for several years. Now Albert discovered that Hélène was one of the few people who seemed to understand what he was about to do. She shared his commitment to helping others.

Hélène gave up her work as a social worker to study nursing, telling Albert that he would need skilled nursing help in the Congo. It was her shy way of proposing marriage.

In October 1911, Albert earned enough money playing at a music festival in Paris to pay the fee for his final medical school exams. On December 17, he learned that he was now a fully qualified doctor of medicine. The following spring he went to Paris for his medical internship. He studied tropical medicine.

On June 18, 1912, he and Hélène Bresslau were married. Albert had written to Dr. Boegner at the Missionary Society of Paris, offering his services in Africa. Amazingly, the society did not want his help.

The Lambaréné hospital is in Gabon, which was known as French Equatorial Africa. To reach Lambaréné, the Schweitzers would land by ship at Port Gentil and then travel one hundred miles (160 km) up the Ogowé River. In the early days supplies from Europe for the hospital took up to six months to arrive.

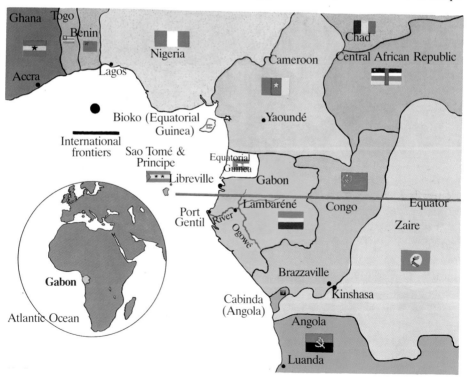

30

The leading members thought that his well-known views on religion, especially on Christ, were simply wrong. Only those who believed every word of the Bible were acceptable to these missionaries. Schweitzer was turned down.

But he wouldn't be defeated. Even before approaching the Missionary Society Committee, he had decided he would raise the money himself to supply a hospital and to finance it for two years.

He became a sort of beggar, writing to every friend he could think of, calling on acquaintances to ask for money for the mission. When he had enough money, he wrote to the Missionary Society, offering to work entirely at his own expense on the Ogowé River at the mission station at Andende near a place called Lambaréné. To his amazement, several leading members of the society still distrusted him, regarding him as a bad Christian. Determined to succeed, Schweitzer called on every one of them individually. Finally, he was accepted, but he had to promise not to preach his faith to the natives of the Congo. He was to work there simply as a doctor. Schweitzer promised he would be "as dumb as a carp."

On Friday, March 21, 1913, he and Hélène boarded a train at the Günsbach railroad station, on the way first to Paris and then to a ship which would take them from Bordeaux, on the west coast of France, to Africa.

When the Schweitzers first went to Africa they were considered to be outstandingly brave — even foolhardy. At the beginning of this century, the jungle was truly dangerous. With poor transportation and no medical facilities, there was a very high death rate among missionaries and other travelers to Africa.

In Africa for the first time

Albert and Hélène Schweitzer arrived at Andende in April 1913. A slower boat with seventy cases of medical supplies arrived later. The climate in this part of Africa was hot, wet, unhealthy, and unwelcoming. In spite of this, as he sailed up the Ogowé River, Schweitzer was overjoyed. Palms and palm trees, roots and creepers projected into the water. Wide fields of papyrus clumps were as tall as a man. Dead giant trees shot up to heaven, their roots rotting below.

"In every gap in the forest a water mirror meets the eye; at every bend in the river a new tributary shows itself. A heron flies heavily up and then settles on a dead tree trunk; white birds and blue birds skim over the water, and high in the air a pair of ospreys circle.

A hollowed-out tree trunk serves as a boat, bringing patients and supplies along the Ogowé River to Schweitzer's hospital at Lambaréné. There was no road to the hospital until 1959.

We are really in Africa!" This was his first delighted impression of the country that was to be his home.

Lambaréné is an island in the middle of the huge Ogowé River, a river filled with crocodiles and hippopotamuses. Not far upriver, at a place called Andende, stood the mission run by the Missionary Society of Paris. Two teachers from the mission welcomed the Schweitzers as they left the ship at Lambaréné. Then the Schweitzers found themselves seated in canoes that were hollowed out of tree trunks and that lay frighteningly low in the water. Paddling them were singing and smiling men from the area.

The chicken-coop hospital

No doctor or nurse had ever worked at Andende, and news of the Schweitzers' coming had already reached the jungle community. Albert, however, was determined not to treat anybody except patients in urgent need of his care, for he needed time to settle in and build a simple hospital. But when he rose the following morning, he found a line of patients already

Opposite: Often patients arrived so undernourished that they needed nutrition before Schweitzer and his team of doctors and nurses could operate on them.

waiting for treatment. The so-called "jungle tele-graph," messages played on tom-toms, had announced that "Oganga — the White Fetishman — has come among us." Albert changed his mind. These people were suffering terrible medical problems. The least serious consisted of snakebites. Malaria, sleeping sickness, pneumonia, the deadly crawling leprosy, ulcers, and tropical skin diseases were much worse. Albert was anxious to relieve the suffering, but work on the hospital hadn't even started. So the Schweitzers asked their teacher friends if there was any building they could rig up as a temporary clinic. All that was available was a filthy chicken coop. Albert and Hélène swept it out, disinfected everywhere, and then began to work in their first jungle hospital.

At first they wanted only to supply medicine and clean up wounds. Soon they had no choice but to operate on a seriously ill patient. Later, Schweitzer wrote: "We must all die," he mused, "but that I can save him from days of torture, that is . . . my great and ever new privilege. Pain is a more terrible lord of mankind than even death himself."

From the start, Schweitzer had had difficulty communicating with the local people. Among his first patients was a cook named Joseph Avzawami, who spoke French. He was an intelligent, articulate young man, so Albert asked Joseph if he would help. Joseph agreed, and he turned out to be a valuable assistant, translating instructions to the patients, advising Albert about how to deal with the patients, and helping at the clinic. He was to stay by Schweitzer's side for fifty years.

Building a hospital

Soon work on the mission hospital began. Albert and Hélène found natives who were happy to work alongside them, building suitable hospital wards, although these were extremely simple by today's standards. By the end of the year, the corrugated-iron building was ready.

The Schweitzers and Joseph were kept busy with the large number of patients. Whenever a patient was treated, the patient's family would arrive and sit patiently outside the jungle hospital, waiting for their relative's recovery.

So that the hospital would run smoothly, Albert introduced "standing orders" on how the patients and their families should behave. Spitting near the hospital was forbidden; those waiting were not to talk to each other loudly; patients and their friends had to take enough food for one day, as they couldn't all be treated early in the day.

The rules were observed, and in return for the medicines and help they received, the patients were expected to give something in return. Gifts of money, eggs, poultry, and bananas were donated to show their appreciation.

The Schweitzers are arrested

On August 5, 1914, the Schweitzers learned that the armies of Germany and France were fighting each other — World War I had started. Albert and Hélène were both Germans working in French territory.

That evening the French authorities told them they were prisoners of war. They were allowed to remain

Top: A rare early photograph of the first hospital.
Above: From the start, patients would arrive with their families.

in their house, but they were not allowed to mix with other people. Armed guards turned Albert's patients away. Fortunately, the authorities recognized the value of the Schweitzers' work, so they were allowed to continue into November.

Albert's relief at being allowed to remain in Lambaréné, at least for the time being, was shattered when he received word that some cavalry officers had galloped around a corner on a road near Günsbach and trampled his mother to death.

The kindness of French authorities did not last. They later told the Schweitzers that they must leave Africa. Both spent much of 1918 as prisoners in a camp in southern France. They were deeply depressed.

When French authorities finally released the Schweitzers in July and allowed them to return to Günsbach, Albert was worn out and ill. Hélène's health was even worse than her husband's. Their imprisonment had ruined the health of both of them. When they were set free, Albert was hardly able to carry their bags. Dysentery had left him with not only a terrible fever that no medicine seemed to cure but also an abscess of the bowel. The pain was horrible. Immediate surgery was vital.

Schweitzer's jungle hospital in the early years. Corrugated-iron roofs later replaced the raffia and bamboo of the older buildings, which soon deteriorated and were not very healthy.

35

The Schweitzers in despair

Albert and Hélène were close to despair. Hélène never recovered enough to be permanently at his side in Africa again. Both had caught dysentery and tuberculosis during imprisonment. Albert recovered, but tuberculosis left Hélène permanently weakened. For the rest of her life she was an invalid.

All their hopes and intentions seemed to have come to nothing. The only ray of hope was the birth of their daughter Rhena on January 14, 1919, Albert's birthday. The violence of war had injured this sensitive man. The senseless death of his mother, the ill health, the failure of his dream for Africa — all overwhelmed him. Schweitzer became deeply, deeply depressed.

It was the lowest point in his life. But he was an energetic, powerful man, who had used every talent to become famous. With this strength, he gradually rebuilt his life. And the suffering became another strength. His compassion for the suffering added a new dimension to his desire to help. It gave him the strength and understanding to fight even harder. It gave him the will to use his fame to oppose violence and war for the rest of his life.

The person who helped Albert back to life was a Swedish man named Nathan Söderblom. Söderblom was the Archbishop of Uppsala. He had read and admired everything that Albert Schweitzer had written. Now he invited him to lecture at the University of Uppsala. Someone seemed again to appreciate the brilliant Schweitzer, even though he was depressed and sick at the time. His strength returned. He started to write new books. He again began rebuilding beautiful organs. Above all, he started to dream of his return to Africa.

Hélène, with baby Rhena, was too ill to go back. The conditions and the heat of the jungle were sometimes too difficult for the fittest of men. It seemed obvious that the Schweitzers could never return. Albert remained quiet about his dream.

It was Hélène who first spoke to him about his returning without her. She had always put the cause first. No sacrifice had been too much for either of them. And now she knew that he had to go on alone.

Opposite: Schweitzer at work at his home in Günsbach, Alsace. Ivy covers the wall and the window looks out onto the foothills of the Vosges Mountains.

In 1924 Albert Schweitzer sits on a log at Lambaréné, flanked by the first two doctors to assist him in his hospital.

Return to Africa

Schweitzer reached Lambaréné for a second time on April 19, 1924. He was forty-nine years old.

The abandoned hospital was ruined. Some buildings had collapsed completely; the roofs of others were leaking. With local workers, Schweitzer rebuilt the hospital, working in the little spare time he had.

By the end of 1925, the hospital had been rebuilt, but Schweitzer soon found it wasn't big enough. An epidemic of dysentery had broken out, and now more than three times as many patients were staying at the hospital. Something had to be done.

Reluctantly, Schweitzer decided to move the hospital to a new site less than two miles away. He chose a plot of ground on the bank of the Ogowé River, near Lambaréné. It was a big project, but one thing pleased him greatly about the prospect of a new hospital. It would be independent — the leaders of the Missionary Society of Paris could no longer forbid him to preach his own views about Jesus to the Africans he served.

By January 1927, part of the new hospital was finished, and patients were transferred from the old hospital. "For the first time since I began to work in Africa," Dr. Schweitzer later said, "my patients were housed as human beings should be."

When, near the close of summer, the hospital was nearly completed, Schweitzer felt he could return home to see Hélène and Rhena. He finally left Lambaréné on July 21.

A life of service

For the rest of his life, Schweitzer would alternate between working in Lambaréné and raising money, giving concerts, and speaking in Europe. In all, Schweitzer made nineteen journeys to Lambaréné. He was busy wherever he was. In Africa, he was the hospital builder, doctor, and chief administrator. In Europe he raised money for what was by now a very large hospital. He gave organ recitals to raise funds, spent time in Günsbach writing his books, and traveled when he could find the time, giving lectures and collecting awards and honorary degrees.

The awards, honorary degrees, and articles of praise came thicker and faster. Many people agreed with the title *Life* magazine bestowed on him — "The Greatest Man in the World."

He was not the first doctor to brave the wilds of "darkest Africa." But perhaps because his simpler books had become best sellers, he became a touchstone, an inspiration for a whole generation. Somehow his sacrifice caught the imagination of millions of people who followed his humanitarian ideals and his principle of reverence for life. Thousands of people — not just doctors and nurses — followed him into service in Africa and other poor regions.

Over the years, he wrote book after book. He was famous, and a leader in three different fields — music, theology, and philosophy. Besides his scholarly works, he wrote simpler, popular books about his life and humanitarian ideals. These were read by millions.

So it was that Schweitzer used the gift of his fame to inspire others to follow his ideals, especially his respect for all forms of life — not just human life — his

"In his prime, Schweitzer worked on a sixteen-hour schedule when he was on tour. His pace was fast and furious, but his immense reserves of energy were such that he could keep going on a minimum of food and sleep. After he had been working until four o'clock one morning a friend said to him, 'You cannot burn a candle at both ends.' But Schweitzer replied, 'Oh yes you can if the candle is long enough.'"
Everett Skillings

understanding of the African peoples and, late in his life, his desire for world peace.

One of the greatest gifts he had been given was his stamina. For fifty years he quietly, steadily built up the hospital, using his strength to serve others.

Hélène's health made helping at Lambaréné out of the question. Also, she had to bring up Rhena, so she stayed behind in Europe. She was to return to Africa several times, but separation meant the Schweitzers were never again as close as they were earlier.

Even so, Hélène never lost their ideal for the jungle hospital. And in 1938, the year before World War II broke out, her fund-raising efforts were vital in saving the hospital. She set off with Rhena on a fund-raising tour of the United States, lecturing about her husband's work at Lambaréné.

World war again

The war against Nazi Germany began in September of the following year. Adolf Hitler's vicious hatred of Jews revolted Albert Schweitzer. Hélène was Jewish, and their daughter was half-Jewish. Nazi policies would have sent Hélène and Rhena to their deaths.

In January 1939, sensing that war was approaching, Schweitzer hurriedly visited Alsace to buy as many drugs, equipment, and other supplies as his hospital could afford. For all of World War II, the trained staff was reduced to Schweitzer himself, two other doctors, and four nurses. In time, it became necessary to send home all but the most seriously ill patients.

Supplies began to run out, until Hélène's work in the United States began to pay off. Generous U.S. citizens started sending medicines and funds across the Atlantic. But crossing the ocean in wartime was a dangerous affair, and the first twenty-eight cases of drugs arrived only in May 1942.

Daily life at Lambaréné

For Schweitzer, wartime life at the jungle hospital remained arduous. "What makes it so difficult to work in this country," he told a friend, "is the terribly hot and moist climate. Here in the low parts of the virgin forest

The hospital at Lambaréné was surrounded by deep, tropical jungle, home to gorillas and wild animals. There were no roads, no shops, none of the comforts of Schweitzer's French home. The heat and humidity proved too much for many of his staff. But Schweitzer's amazing stamina never failed him. He could manage on just four hours of sleep a night and even in his eighties he would commonly work a sixteen-hour day.

41

Lambaréné became a major hospital, coping with up to a thousand patients a day. This meant an extensive building schedule. Schweitzer not only organized all the building work, but every day, he would spend time on the most menial jobs. It was one of Schweitzer's fundamental beliefs that no one was too superior or too important for the most humble tasks.

it is worst." He added, "I have the splendid privilege, for which I thank God every day, that I can stand the climate fairly well, but some of my co-workers suffer much from it."

At Lambaréné, the dogged doctor continued to build additions to his hospital and to play his beloved Bach. As a present to Schweitzer, the Paris Bach Society had shipped a piano with pedals resembling those of an organ.

Throughout his life, this great man remained humble, even shy. In 1951, to a distinguished French correspondent, Schweitzer wrote, "Tell no one that I am coming to France, for my return is still a secret. I must try to have several weeks of tranquillity at Günsbach to concentrate totally on my writing." Again, he wrote in his hesitant English, "I suffer to be

famous and try to avoid everything which draws more attention to me."

After repeated famines Schweitzer created a large hospital vegetable garden. Year after year, the heavy rains washed away the fertile soil, which then had to be renewed. But eventually all the staff and over one thousand patients a day could be fed from this garden.

He begged an admirer not to visit him in the jungle, adding, "Please let me be as I am, someone who lives and works in silence."

He needed to protect his hospital. Intruders who might photograph or write anything that he considered to be critical were not welcome at Lambaréné. He became increasingly sensitive about questions of publicity, more and more shunning visitors, but at the same time being careful not to avoid the limelight altogether, for his hospital always needed money.

Everyone who came to visit him in Africa was roped into work. In 1947 two U.S. citizens visited the hospital at Lambaréné. "The weeks we spent at Lambaréné were among the most memorable of our lives,"

43

The doctor as laborer. Much of the physical work at Lambaréné was undertaken by Schweitzer himself. For years — until he could afford a truck and a jeep — this wheelbarrow was the hospital's only vehicle.

they later wrote. "We were not mere spectators of a miracle of mercy. We were generously admitted as members of the hospital family. We walked and talked, ate and worked, with Albert Schweitzer. We were assigned our little portion of the responsibility. We were permitted to share the problems, the anxieties, the hopes, the plans, the dreams of this extraordinary jungle doctor."

The comical-looking hero

They found that their hero was a comical-looking man who scarcely ever brushed his thick hair. He wore ancient baggy trousers that had been darned again and again. His pockets bulged with letters. His mustache was thick and as uncombed as his hair. He shaved without soap because he considered soap a luxury. An old sun helmet, covered with a white cloth, was usually pushed back from his forehead. Once, one of his devoted nurses, Emmy Martin, bought him a new hat, but Schweitzer refused to wear it, preferring his old one. His shirts, too, were repaired over and over again.

When he had become famous and had to visit Europe, he traveled third class only because "there was no fourth class." When he went to receive prizes, to give organ recitals, to beg for money for his jungle hospital, he managed with an old black suit, made for him in 1905 by the tailor of the village where he was brought up, and a clip-on bow tie. He would carry his clip-on tie in his pocket. Only when he came near the place where he was to speak or seek money would he put it on. After the occasion, he would take it off with a sigh of relief!

Schweitzer's clothes became one of his trademarks. Often, his shirts and trousers were more patches than original material. "Anything I spend on myself," he said, "I can't spend on my Africans."

To visitors it seemed that this unpretentious man liked animals even more than humans, apart from children. The local people knew that he would care for any sick animal they brought him. As a result, whenever he walked across the courtyard of the jungle hospital, a half-dozen dogs, wagging their tails, would follow him.

He had a pet pig that was so bristly that he would use it to clean the mud off his boots, and he even tamed a pelican. In the evenings he would feed a shy pet owl with little pieces of meat. A pet porcupine, he said, used to dance when he played his piano. And on every veranda there were roaming monkeys.

Schweitzer at work

Then late at night, Schweitzer would work in his little office-bedroom, sitting at an unvarnished table that was half-eaten by termites, working on his latest book — the third volume of his *Philosophy of Civilization*.

He had his own quaint way of writing these remarkable books, working far into the night. If a whole chapter was finished, he would tie the pages together with string and pile them on the shelf above his head. If he was still working on a chapter, the pages he had already written would be hung on string from nails hammered into the wooden walls of the hut.

"I opened the bundle. Here, for all I knew, was one of the most important books of our time. The sheets had been perforated at the top and were tied together by a string. But I gasped when I saw the kind of paper that had been used for the manuscript. There were sheets of every size and description. Dr. Schweitzer had written his book in longhand on the reverse side of miscellaneous papers. Some of them were outdated tax forms . . . some came from old calendars. I couldn't even count the number of pages which were written on the reverse sides of letters . . ."
From Albert Schweitzer's
Mission, *by Norman Cousins*

45

Mail poured into Lambaréné from all over the world. Schweitzer took time to answer it all. And he left time for his own pleasures as well. In the evenings, Bach's music would ring throughout the hospital as Schweitzer played his piano with pedals.

Visitors who spent time with Schweitzer would be amazed at his high spirits and good mood. "One would never suppose that he had only three hours' sleep last night and only four hours' sleep the night before," a visitor once recalled. "Last night he worked on his correspondence and his papers until after midnight, spent two hours in the delivery room with the woman who was having her baby, and as usual got up at six."

At the age of seventy, Schweitzer himself was amazed that he was still able to work so well. "It is a grace," he said.

Albert Schweitzer reads a letter from an admirer. Countless people wrote to him. "My paperwork is killing me," he once complained. "Week by week the mail gets larger." Another time he joked, "Long after I am dead I feel I shall still be answering letters."

Reverence for life

Schweitzer loved Africa's animals. He made pets of monkeys and, above all, he adored his pelican. More and more, he came to revere every form of life. Human beings, he taught, had no right to exploit or ravage the animal kingdom.

"We owe our birth to the life of others," he wrote. "We can give life to others. Thus nature forces us to acknowledge the fact that our life finds itself in solidarity with other lives."

Schweitzer had first worked out this idea of reverence for life as he sailed on the Ogowé River in September 1915. "Late on the third day, at the very moment when, at sunset, we were making our way through a herd of hippopotamuses, there flashed upon my mind, unforeseen and unsought, the phrase 'Reverence for Life.'"

Every night Schweitzer would play Bach on his piano. This brought him not only a continuing sense of joy and peace but also the ability to give highly acclaimed recitals back in Europe.

Now he wrote that the greatest good is to preserve life, to promote life, to raise life to the highest value that it is capable of. "The greatest evil is to destroy life, to injure life, to repress life which is capable of development." So, he argued, life itself — all life — is sacred, and we only become decent beings when we recognize this. This was the principle on which his whole philosophy was based.

All this he put into practice at Lambaréné. Next to the large number of huts and barracks for sick people, he built a group of stables for sick animals. A dog belonging to a lumber camp manager near Lambaréné had gotten a bone stuck in his throat. Schweitzer performed an operation to remove it. A chimpanzee had a gangrenous arm that had to be amputated by Dr. Walter Munz, one of Schweitzer's assistants. The chimp later became a roommate.

At one time, Schweitzer wrote to a friend, the hospital sheltered 250 sheep and goats. "They are not killed. They will die a natural death. We have a pelican which lodges in a tree opposite my room. His friends are a goat and its child.

"Poor dogs abandoned by the natives find their way to the hospital and stay with us. The dogs and monkeys make friends. At this moment we have five chimpanzees and eight ordinary monkeys." He added that this way of life arose from his own teaching of reverence for life.

Schweitzer's sick pelican

This did not mean that he regarded all forms of life as equal. One of his assistants was irritated by Dr. Schweitzer's reverence for life until one day when he saw the great doctor's beloved pelican stuggling to land. One leg was hanging down limply, and the pelican vainly tried to land again and again. Finally the bird crashed to a halt. The doctor sent a message to Schweitzer: "Tell Dr. Schweitzer that his pelican has a broken leg." An hour later Schweitzer came in and asked, "Do you have a moment? I would like you to come and consult with me about my pelican." The assistant answered, "Doctor, I come." But Schweitzer replied, "No — your patients first."

Schweitzer named his pelican Parsifal. By day it swam in the river or flew into the jungle, but each night it always returned. Schweitzer wrote a book, supposedly in the pelican's own words, in which Parsifal says, "I swore that the doctor would not easily shake me off."

The assistant was pleased that Dr. Schweitzer had established priorities for medical treatment. No matter what, animals took second place to humans.

How far did Schweitzer allow his problems to affect his faith in reverence for life? The answer is — not at all. In 1960 he wrote to a correspondent who wanted to know what his life's philosophy was: "All that I have to say to the world and to mankind is contained in the notion, reverence for life."

As he grew older Schweitzer became convinced that this respect for all life should drive people to become vegetarians. As he put it, "The great problem whether we ought to kill and eat animals is slowly becoming clear to us. There is much to be said against it." His view was "to join the movement to protect

"We have invented many things, but we have not mastered the creation of life. We cannot even create an insect."
Albert Schweitzer

Every day after dinner Schweitzer would fill his pockets with crusts and go to the antelope pen, where the animals would rush to him and lick the salty sweat from his arms before being fed.

The sick thronged his hospital. They brought their whole families and often livestock as well, setting up home on the hospital grounds until their sick ones were healed. The informality and chaos caused sharp criticism from some overseas visitors who expected to see sterile white wards.

beasts, and to renounce and speak against the consumption of meat." He regretted that he had not done so earlier. The Bible had not seen it as a problem, nor had most philosophers, but he felt it to be a matter of the deepest importance for humanity.

The people of Africa

As Schweitzer had warmed to his life in French Equatorial Africa, he had spotted the fine qualities of a good number of black men and women. As he remarked, these are "native Christians who are in every respect thoroughly moral personalities." One was

Oyembo, the schoolmaster, who taught in the Lambaréné boys' school. His name meant "the song."

Schweitzer wrote, "I look upon him as one of the finest men that I know anywhere," adding that "probably no one has ever borne so beautiful a name more worthily than this black teacher." Oyembo was clever, kindly, and modest. "There was something so refined about him that one felt almost shy in his presence."

A kind but often short-tempered white trader once said to Dr. Schweitzer, "What a good thing it is that the Negroes have better characters than we have." Schweitzer decided that there was probably much truth in the trader's opinion.

He himself could lose his temper with his assistants, and he remembered the way they patiently put up with this. "They quietly went on with their work," he wrote, "and remained as friendly as if they had never had to endure our probably . . . excessive abuse." He recognized, too, that the life of these black men and women was hard, especially for those who lived in the forest where there was always danger, little food, and almost no sun.

He remained a devout Christian and enriched his beliefs by learning from those who believed in religions other than his own. Africa broadened his mind.

"There are scores of Africans with all sorts of maladies. I went down among them with the Doctor one day. It was lovely to see his tenderness, his concern, his closeness to them in spirit."
Dr. Emory Ross, of the Albert Schweitzer Fellowship

Justice in the jungle

Schweitzer also sensitively acknowledged the virtues of what he called "primitive tribal justice," justice administered locally and swiftly by the tribal chief. By contrast, Europeans who attempted to administer justice, either infrequently or from far away, did not understand the lives of the witnesses and couldn't speak their languages. So the judges were bound to be slow and inefficient — especially when they were, as Schweitzer said, "immature, untested and inexperienced white men, exasperated beyond expression by the ways of primitive men."

Schweitzer admired many Africans, but he did not have a good opinion of those Europeans who had colonized Africa. He believed many of them were there simply to make money at the expense of the black people. "We, the Christian nations, send out

51

Opposite: The landing stage at Lambaréné, with dugout canoes moored outside the hospital. Patients came hundreds of miles by river. Those who were not able to walk were put onto stretchers and taken to Schweitzer's clinic.

there the mere dregs of our people," he once wrote. "We think only of what we can get out of the natives."

The worst thing of all was the way the white people had developed the slave trade, transporting black Africans to North America and the West Indies, bribing black leaders to sell their own people. Slaves were often exchanged for salt or rum, and sometimes the parents were drowned and only the children sold. Almost always, once a family was sold into slavery, the parents and children were split up, never to see each other again.

Of the estimated twelve million black slaves transported to America, another two million or so are calculated to have died in the evil conditions they were forced to endure on the way there.

Exploitation

He believed strongly that whites had wickedly exploited blacks and were still doing so. In 1928 he set out his views on colonialism and white exploitation of blacks in a powerful article called "The Relations of the White and Colored Races."

When white people reached the colonies, Schweitzer argued, the black people were at risk. From the moment the first white person's boat arrived with powder, rum, salt, or fabrics on the shores of what were called "primitive or semi-primitive peoples," the black people lost their independence, their way of life turned upside-down, and their chiefs tempted to sell their people for material goods.

He remained certain that most European people had treated Africans with utter selfishness. Large white cities had been built around small primitive villages, forcing the villagers to move without careful planning and adequate warning, not to speak of frequent violence.

Thinking about the Africans' right to education, Schweitzer passionately asked, "When the modern state talks about doing an educational work among the natives, I say to it: 'Do not make phrases; show me your work. How many educators have you in fact exported to your colony?'"

Albert and Hélène Schweitzer together at Lambaréné in 1957, shortly before her death. Albert appreciated her presence: "She keeps going all day long and her help is very precious."

Albert Schweitzer in a Swedish church, listening attentively to organ music.

Atomic bombs

Schweitzer boldly invited criticism when it came to matters of world importance. After World War II and throughout the last twenty years of his life, he became more and more troubled by the threat to peace from the invention of the atomic bomb. Nothing caused him more anguish and brought him more criticism in his final years than his attempts to bring about a safer world by persuading governments to give up nuclear weapons. Even testing nuclear weapons, he warned, would send dangerous radioactive material into the skies, and this material was certain to affect the health of people yet to be born.

This crusader for peace warned, "Only those who have never been present at the birth of a deformed baby, never witnessed the whimpering shock of its mother, dare to maintain that the risk in going on with nuclear tests is one which must be taken under existing circumstances." The great powers did not like Schweitzer's remarks about their frightful weapons. Some members of the Western press ceased to praise him and began to attack him. The doctor was bruised but undaunted.

The Nobel Prize

In October 1953, aged seventy-eight, Albert Schweitzer was awarded the Nobel Peace Prize. He used the prize money to build a village for leprosy sufferers at Lambaréné. He went to Oslo to give the Nobel lecture. Schweitzer took the opportunity to make a powerful plea for peace. He claimed to be speaking the innermost hopes and thoughts of millions of people who were living in fear of the next war. And he bitingly attached those statesmen who after each war had wrecked the possibility of creating a society that would promote harmony and prosperity.

From 1914 on, he pointed out, governments had been developing increasingly horrible methods of attacking their enemies. Planes allowed them to rain bombs from above. Then human beings, posing as supermen, developed yet greater means of savagery, a process that continued far beyond their dreams when they discovered that the atom could be split. He warned, "Let those who hold the fates of peoples in their hands be careful to avoid everything which may worsen our situation and make it more perilous."

Increasingly he felt that "the beginning of the end" of the human race was approaching. Modern science had placed too many powers of destruction in the hands of people who did not handle it responsibly. The process begun in World War I had grown worse as atomic research put massively dangerous weapons into the hands of weak people. To Schweitzer, total disaster seemed near. He felt we must dedicate ourselves to one supreme aim of life, to become "simpler, more truthful, purer, more peace-loving, meeker, kinder, more sympathetic" toward our fellow human beings and all creation.

Many of the world's universities — Edinburgh, Oxford, Tübingen, Yale, Cambridge — showered degrees on the great Dr. Schweitzer.

Schweitzer toils for world peace

Here Schweitzer brought into his Nobel Peace Prize speech one of the permanent themes of his life's thought. The question did not simply concern the future of humanity. It concerned something more far-reaching — Earth itself and every life form that Earth sustains and nurtures.

Nuclear war could destroy far more than human beings. So, he said, the compassion extended to human beings must be extended to every living thing.

Opposing nuclear weapons stemmed from a reverence for all life. Schweitzer concluded that in any atomic war, losses resulting from bombardment would

Schweitzer often returned to sit quietly in the fields above his Günsbach home in the Münster valley. "Nature spoke to me here when I was small, before I went to school," he remembered, "in the vineyards which my father had planted, among the rocks. . . ."

not result in victory but in catastrophe. Finally, Schweitzer introduced his own particular element into his speech: the notion of mutual trust.

If governments did not trust one another, the only hope for an agreement to ban nuclear tests lay in some neutral organization. This organization would have the job of investigating the nuclear activities of all nations capable of developing and using nuclear energy.

While much could be achieved by such a body, it would never be enough. It could guarantee only temporary safety, temporary peace. This is because governments themselves are temporary: "Governments can change and the production and testing of atomic weapons [can be] resumed."

So for Schweitzer there could never be an acceptable substitute for trust. The solution to the nuclear threat could be achieved for all time, he argued, "only . . . if there is a surge of public opinion in the East and in the West condemning atomic weapons."

Abolishing nuclear weapons

At last an agreement banning nuclear tests was reached. Yet Schweitzer, now over eighty, still campaigned for lasting peace. He saw the agreement as only a beginning. He insisted that "the sun can rise only when nuclear test explosions altogether cease."

Next, the large quantities of nuclear weapons already stockpiled needed dismantling — "abolishing," as Schweitzer expressed it. But he did not see how such a project, indispensable as it was for world peace, could be completely supervised or controlled.

So Schweitzer returned to his own special contribution to the nuclear debate — the need to work for mutual trust among people. "One government can be replaced by another government," he pointed out, "but the people remain and their will is decisive. The people themselves must take a stand."

But could this ever happen? Schweitzer's faith insisted that it might be possible, if only men and women would listen to God's demands. "Belief in the kingdom of God makes the biggest demands of all the articles of the Christian faith," Schweitzer held. "It means believing the seemingly impossible —

Schweitzer, the man of vision, determined to serve. "The only way out of today's misery is for people to become worthy of each other's trust," he declared.

the conquest of the spirit of the world by the spirit of God." He added: "The miracle must happen in us before it can happen in the world."

Inspire in individual human beings the need for peace and the need for mutual trust, he suggested, and one will eventually be able to influence governments.

The last journey to Lambaréné

During all these last years of activity, including visits to Europe and the United States to collect awards and to raise money, Schweitzer missed the hospital. During his last visit to Europe, his friend Jacques Feschotte listened to him playing the organ one evening. Then they sat together on Schweitzer's bench. "It'll be quiet at Lambaréné too," the doctor said. "There'll be a sleepy feeling in all the huts, except where the people cry out in pain. All the animals are asleep. Doctors and nurses are hoping to get some rest. Yes, it's exactly the same moment in the day."

Schweitzer's death

In December 1959, Albert Schweitzer made his final journey to Lambaréné. He was now almost eighty-five. He wanted to spend what remained of his life in Lambaréné and eventually to be buried there, alongside Hélène, who had died in 1957.

Lambaréné: The graves of Albert and Hélène Schweitzer, marked by simple wooden crosses.

During these final years Schweitzer received visitors from all over the world. He also corresponded, wrote books, helped run the hospital, fed the animals, and played his beloved Bach.

And, quietly, on September 4, 1965, this great man died. He was ninety years old.

His last walk through the hospital grounds had been delightful; he said goodbye to every tree he had planted. When he was buried, the little bag of rice that he used to carry to feed the chickens, along with his battered old hat, were placed in his coffin.

For weeks afterward, groups of black men, women, and children gathered to pay their last respects to the jungle doctor. One of his fellow workers described how one morning she "woke at six o'clock to the singing of children and adults; for half an hour they sang, expressing their love and gratitude. It moved me thoroughly, and I thought of the doctor, how this would touch him in his soul. Once a native said to him, 'When you die we will have a tom-tom of a week to mourn you.' The doctor jokingly replied, 'Fortunately I won't hear it.'"

No Gift Is Too Small

Just as one sound can sometimes cause a disastrous avalanche and one tiny, tumbling pebble can start a rock slide, one small, thoughtful act can snowball into a great outpouring of generosity.

This occurred when the charitable gesture of one young man caused many citizens of Europe to donate thousands of dollars to support Schweitzer's work in Lambaréné.

In 1959, Robert Hill, age thirteen, learned about the work of Schweitzer in Africa and decided that even though he was just a boy, he wanted to help. So this enterprising young man from Georgia wrote to a man he'd heard about, Lieutenant General Richard Lindsay of the U.S. Air Force, who was then stationed in Italy. Robert thought that perhaps Lindsay would be close enough to the Belgian Congo to do him a favor.

Robert wondered — could Lindsay carry a bottle of aspirin on his plane and could he drop it carefully from the air as he flew over Schweitzer's hospital at Lambaréné?

Italian newspapers heard about Robert's plan. They made an appeal in both Italy and France, asking that

Robert Hill, age 13, meets Albert Schweitzer on July 31, 1959*

the Italian and French people be at least as generous as Robert Hill. This appeal was to raise $400,000 before it ended, aid in the form of medical supplies and much-needed capital.

These supplies were then flown to Schweitzer in the Congo, to be used by Schweitzer and his assistants in the jungle hospital.

Robert Hill's bottle of aspirin was not on that flight and never was dropped from the plane. Instead, Hill himself was given a free ride to the Congo to meet Schweitzer in person. He hand-delivered his bottle of aspirin and shyly received Schweitzer's sincere thanks.

*Picture courtesy of Paul Popper Photo

For More Information . . .

Organizations

Write to the organizations below if you want to learn more about Albert Schweitzer and about subjects related to medicine, such as current medical and health issues, medical missions, and careers in medicine. You may also want to know more about Johann Sebastian Bach, the composer Schweitzer deeply admired. Some of these groups may have publications that you could subscribe to. When you write, be sure to tell them exactly what you want to know, and include your name, address, and age.

Albert Schweitzer Center
Hurlburt Road, R. D. 1, Box 7
Great Barrington, MA 01230

Albert Schweitzer Fellowship
866 United Nations Plaza
New York, NY 10017

American Bach Foundation
1211 Potomac Street NW
Washington, DC 20007

American Medical Association
535 N. Dearborn Street
Chicago, IL 60610

American Nurses' Association
2420 Pershing Road
Kansas City, MO 64108

International Health Society
1001 E. Oxford Lane
Cherry Hills Village
Englewood, CO 80110

National Health Council
622 Third Ave., 34th Floor
New York, NY 10017

World Medical Missions
P. O. Box 3000
Boone, NC 28607

Books

The books listed below will help you learn more about Albert Schweitzer and his many interests, including music, philosophy, medicine in underdeveloped countries, and world peace. Check at your local library or bookstore to see if they have them or can order them for you.

About Albert Schweitzer —

Albert Schweitzer. Cremaschi (Silver Burdett)
Albert Schweitzer. Schweitzer (Repath, editor) (Creative Education)
Albert Schweitzer: Genius in the Jungle. Gollomb (Vanguard)
All Men Are Brothers: A Portrait of Albert Schweitzer. Simon (Dutton)
Dr. Schweitzer of Lambaréné. Cousins (Dutton)

About Africa —

Africa. Thomas (Fideler)
Along the Niger River: An African Way of Life. Jenness (Crowell Jr.)
Famine in Africa. Timberlake (Franklin Watts)
Lost Freedom. Kaufmann (Astor-Honor)
The Sign of the Ivory Horn: Eastern African Civilizations. Rosenthal (Oceana)

About Johann Sebastian Bach, Other Composers, and Music —

Bach. Millar (Silver Burdett)
Lives of Great Composers. Woodward (Merry Thoughts)
Story of Music. Mundy (Usborne-Hayes)
Women of Notes. Laurence (Rosen Group)

About World Peace and Peacemakers —

Challenge of Peace. Sibley & Sibley (Dillon)
Learning Peace. Abrams and Schmidt (Women's International League for Peace and Freedom)
The Peace Seekers: The Nobel Peace Prize. Aaseng (Lerner)
Peacemakers: Informing the World. North (Dillon)

Magazines

The following magazines will give you more information about health and about events occurring among peoples and nations around the world. Check your library to see if they have these magazines, or write to the addresses listed below to get information about subscribing.

Current Events and *Current Science*
4343 Equity Drive
Columbus, OH 43228

Current Health 1
P.O. Box 6991
Syracuse, NY 13217

Faces
P.O. Box 3060
Northbrook, IL 60065

OWL
P.O. Box 11314
Des Moines, IA 50340

Junior Scholastic
In the United States
P.O. Box 644
Lyndhurst, NJ 07071-9985

. . . and in Canada
Richmond Hill, Ontario
Canada   L4C 3G5

Glossary

Alsace

An area along the Rhine, now in eastern France, which was in dispute between France and Germany for many years. It changed hands several times. The Alsatians speak both French and German. The area is not only beautiful but also notable for its white wines, made from the high-quality grapes grown there.

Amputate

To cut off a part of the body, usually an arm or leg, because it is too badly damaged by accident or disease to heal.

Anesthetic

A substance that causes loss of bodily sensation. A local anesthetic numbs just the area that is to be treated, while a general anesthetic causes the patient to lose consciousness. This allows a surgeon to operate without causing pain to the patient.

Atonement

To reconcile; to perform some definite action in order to make up for an injury or wrong done to another person or people. In Christianity, Christ's life and death are considered the atonement that serves to reconcile God and man.

Bach, Johann Sebastian (1685-1750)

One of the greatest European composers, he spent most of his life in what is now East Germany. He wrote nearly two hundred cantatas, oratorios, and masses, two Passions, the six Brandenburg Concertos, and many pieces for the organ. Because his type of music went out of fashion, he was almost forgotten for nearly a century. Schweitzer's book on how to perform Bach's works was important in gaining Bach's rightful recognition.

Fetish

An object that is believed to contain magical powers or to be the home of a spirit that a person can call upon for help. Also used to describe extreme attention to something. For example, one could be said to have a fetish about neatness. Also spelled *fetich*.

Fingering

The technique used in playing an instrument so that the music flows without pauses as the musician repositions the hands. For very complicated organ music, people can spend years trying to figure out different ways of fingering.

Gabon, Republic of

An area lying in western central Africa. Colonized by the French in 1839, it became part of the French Congo in 1888. It received independence in 1960 but remains part of the French community of states. The national language is French. Its main products are oil and timber; the country is still mostly forest. As of 1988, the population is estimated at just over a million.

Gangrene

The condition that occurs when the blood supply to a part of the body is cut off and the part deprived begins to die. The flesh turns black, begins to rot, and emits a terrible sickly smell. The only cure is to cut off the part that is affected.

Hernia

A severe overstraining of the wall of the abdomen that causes the muscle lining that holds the intestines in position to tear. This allows part of the intestine to bulge out through the hole.

Humanitarian

A person whose chief goal is to promote human welfare and social programs; a philanthropist. Someone called a humanitarian is more likely to focus on the well-being of all people rather than special groups.

Improvisation

In musical terms, to compose on an instrument as you go along. Often a musician can develop an improvisation from a bit of tune, without having any idea where the piece is going to finish. Schweitzer was extremely good at this sort of composing.

Knacker's yard

A place where horses bought for their meat are kept before being killed. The odors and insects common to these areas make them very unpleasant places.

Leprosy

Also known as Hansen's Disease, leprosy attacks the nervous system so that all feeling is lost from the parts affected. Often, the parts have to be amputated. Now we can cure leprosy by using various drugs. Found primarily in tropical areas, it is not very infectious. About twelve million people in the world are afflicted today.

Malaria

An infectious disease caused by the bite of the *Anopheles* mosquito. Its symptoms are alternate shivering and fever. Malaria is hard to cure; the drugs must be taken for some time, even after patients leave the malarial area.

Missionary

A person sent by a religious organization to do religious and social work in a foreign, usually underdeveloped, country. Some missionaries take religious vows.

Philosophy

The word derives from the Greek roots *philos*, "love of," and *sophos*, "wisdom." Philosophy is the study of everything humans have known and can know. People approach the study of philosophy by both examining the work of the great philosophers and contributing their own ideas.

Reverence

An attitude or feeling of deep respect for someone or something. Schweitzer evolved a philosophy of "reverence for life" that required him to respect, as if it were human, all life on Earth – whether plant or animal.

Sleeping sickness
Popular name for a disease caused by the bite of the tsetse fly. Its symptoms are fever, which may last for up to three years, followed by sluggish behavior and wasting of the muscles. It is mostly found in Africa and parts of tropical America.

Theology
The study of God, his nature, and the way he relates to the world, through reading holy books and the works of important thinkers in the subject. In Schweitzer's time, it was usually studied in relation to one religion, such as Christianity, Hinduism, Islam, or Judaism, for example.

Widor, Charles Marie (1845-1937)
Born in Lyons, in France, he became the organist at St. Sulpice in Paris in 1869, a prestigious position. In 1891, Widor became professor of organ at the Paris Conservatory. Among his compositions were ten symphonies for the organ and many other works featuring this instrument.

Chronology

1875   **January 14** — Albert Schweitzer born in Kaysersberg, Upper Alsace.
Summer — The Schweitzers move to Günsbach.

1884   Schweitzer, only nine years old, begins playing the organ in his father's church in the village of Günsbach. In the following years, he develops his skill in music.

1885   Schweitzer goes to boarding school at Mülhausen.

1890   Schweitzer first comes across the works of J. S. Bach.

1893   Schweitzer enters the University of Strasbourg and plans to study theology and philosophy. He studies organ under Widor in Paris.

1899   At Strasbourg, Schweitzer publishes *Kant's Philosophy of Religion*, an acclaimed work on an extremely difficult philosopher. It earns him his Doctorate of Philosophy.
December — He is appointed pastor of St. Nicholas Church in Strasbourg.

1900   Schweitzer earns a licentiate in theology. He becomes the Principal of the Theological College of St. Thomas at the University of Strasbourg.

1903   Schweitzer becomes principal of his college in Strasbourg.

1904   A magazine article persuades Schweitzer to become a medical missionary.

1905   Schweitzer resigns from his college and begins training as a doctor of medicine at Strasbourg. He publishes his best-known musicological work, *Johann Sebastian Bach.*

1906   Schweitzer publishes *The Quest for the Historical Jesus* and a book on how to build organs.

1911   Schweitzer finishes his medical studies. To raise money for his licensing examination fee, he begins giving recitals. He also gives recitals to raise money to build a hospital in central Africa.

1912   **June 18** — Schweitzer marries Hélène Bresslau, who has completed nurse's training in order to be of help to Schweitzer at the medical mission.

1913   The Schweitzers sail for Africa with two thousand francs in gold and medical supplies. Schweitzer opens his jungle hospital at Lambaréné.

1914   World War I begins. French authorities intern the Schweitzers because they are German subjects. Their health fails dramatically.

1917   The Schweitzers are deported to France as prisoners of war. Albert treats the other prisoners in the internment camp. His mother is killed by a German cavalry officer.

1918   The Schweitzers are released to Switzerland.
November 11— World War I ends as the warring nations sign an armistice in France.

1919   **January 14** — The Schweitzers' daughter, Rhena, is born.

1920   Schweitzer publishes *On the Edge of the Primeval Forest* and begins lecturing and giving organ concerts so that he can raise enough money to return to Lambaréné.

1923   Schweitzer publishes his two-volume *Philosophy of Civilization.*

1924   Schweitzer reaches Lambaréné and finds it in ruins. Hélène and Rhena remain in Europe for health reasons.

1925   An outbreak of amoebic dysentery forces Schweitzer to move the hospital to a new site.

1927-39   Schweitzer frequently visits Europe in order to raise money for the hospital.

1930   Schweitzer publishes *The Mysticism of Paul the Apostle* and, the next year, publishes his autobiography, *Out of My Life and Thought.*

1932 In a speech at Frankfurt, Germany, Schweitzer warns of the dangers of Nazism and a second world war.

1935 Schweitzer publishes *Indian Thought and Its Development.*

1939 **September 1** — World War II begins. Knowing the dangers in Europe, Schweitzer no longer visits Europe. Hélène joins him in Africa in 1941.

1945 World War II ends.

1950-52 Schweitzer tours many countries, giving concerts and speaking out against nuclear weapons.

1952 Schweitzer is awarded the Nobel Peace Prize. He uses the money to build a village for three hundred people with leprosy.

1955 Schweitzer is awarded Britain's Order of Merit. He becomes the second non-British person to win this prestigious award.

1957 Hélène Schweitzer dies in Zurich, Switzerland, and is buried at Lambaréné.

1965 **September 4** — Schweitzer dies at Lambaréné. He is buried in a simple wooden coffin next to his wife.

1967 Schweitzer's *The Kingdom of God and Primitive Christianity* is published.

1976 The hospital at Lambaréné is rebuilt because buildings have become old, shabby, and inadequate for patient care.

1981 **January** — A modern hospital opens at Lambaréné.

Index